Nice Things

A Queer Love Story

Luke Hereford

methuen | drama

LONDON • NEW YORK • OXFORD • NEW DELHI • SYDNEY

METHUEN DRAMA
Bloomsbury Publishing Plc, 50 Bedford Square, London, WC1B 3DP, UK
Bloomsbury Publishing Inc, 1359 Broadway, New York, NY 10018, USA
Bloomsbury Publishing Ireland, 29 Earlsfort Terrace, Dublin 2,
D02 AY28, Ireland

First published in Great Britain 2026

Photograph and designer: Aled Wyn Thomas

A catalogue record for this book is available from the British Library.

A catalog record for this book is available from the Library of Congress.

ISBN: PB: 978-1-3506-3374-2
ePDF: 978-1-3506-3375-9
eBook: 978-1-3506-3376-6

Series: Modern Plays

Typeset by Mark Heslington Ltd, Scarborough, North Yorkshire

For product safety related questions contact productsafety@bloomsbury.com.

To find out more about our authors and books visit www.bloomsbury.com and sign up for our newsletters.

NICE THINGS: A QUEER LOVE STORY PROGRAMME NOTES

'he/him/they/them/him/they/he/us/you/I don't know/how do you keep getting this wrong?'

NICE THINGS: A QUEER LOVE STORY finds a gay couple, in the midst of their comfortable years. The two of them have everything; a beautiful flat, three holidays a year and truly envious instagram grids. Nothing could ripple their idealistic world. Except for each other. When one of them comes out as nonbinary, their idealised gay picket fence life begins to crumble.

How do we deal with drastic changes in someone we love apparently unconditionally? Are they really that drastic? Does it actually change anything? And isn't it better if your partner is just themself? Isn't that what you love about them? Maybe. But maybe not that much themself.

Previous praise for *Grandmother's Closet* by Luke Hereford:

'Lovely, funny, touching' ★★★★★ Musical Theatre Review

'Infectiously entertaining...moving and meaningful' ★★★★ Stage

'Exuberant and heartwarming' ★★★★ Scotsman

NICE THINGS: A Queer Love Story is Porter's Theatre first official co-production, and is made possible with support from Arts Council of Wales, sponsored by Welsh Government.

NICE THINGS: A Queer Love Story originally premiered at the Pleasance Theatre, London 1 – 4 April 2026 before transferring to Porter's Theatre for its Cardiff run 22 – 25 April 2026.

Original cast

He	Geraint Rhys Edwards
They	Reece Connolly

Director	Izzy Rabey
Designer	Cara Evans
Lighting Designer	Marty Langthorne
Sound Designer	Barbs Dudek
Intimacy Coordinator	Emma Weissensteiner
Assistant Director	Eugenia Taylor
Stage Manager	Maia Thompson
Marketing Advisor	Craig Bates
Set Construction	Thomas White & Edward Selwood

CAST

THEY – Reece Connolly *(they/he)*; is a performer, writer and producer from the North East, based in East London. They're also the co-creator and emcee of *The Gallifrey Cabaret*, alongside various other queer geeky variety shows and events which have toured around the UK. As a writer, Reece has been part of two Royal Court Writers' Groups, received an Elevator Festival bursary from the Live Theatre, and in 2018 became the Customs House inaugural Young Writer-in-Residence. At time of writing, they are also one of the six playwrights forming the Oxford Playhouse's 2025–26 Playmakers programme. Other selected performance and writing credits include *It's Behind Who!* (HOME/Wales Millennium Centre)*; Sucker 4 U* (The Pleasance); *Ghosts Of Metroland* (Live Theatre); *Antichristmas* (Laurels); *Wormtown* (The Customs House/Alphabetti Theatre); *Last Orders* (Old Red Lion); *Chutney* (The Bunker); *A Fistful Of Hunny* (theSpaceUK).

HE – Geraint Rhys Edwards *(he/him)*; is from Cardiff and is a native Welsh speaker. He graduated from Rose Bruford College of Theatre and Performance with a BA (Hons); in Acting. Theatre work includes: *Mother Goose* (The Courtyard Theatre); *Sleeping Beauty* (The Courtyard Theatre); *Charlie and the Chocolate Factory* (Aberystwyth Arts Centre); *Feral Monster* (National Theatre Wales); *Brassed Off* (Aberystwyth Arts Centre); *Cinderella* (Riverfront); *Robin Hood* (Riverfront); *Y Cylch Sialc* (Theatr Genedlaethol Cymru); *The White Feather* (Theatr Na'nog); *Myths and Legends*, *A Cowardly Night*, *Berlin Nights* (Bridlington Rep Theatre); *Emperors New Clothes* (Sherman Theatre); *Robin Hood* (Theatre Royal Stratford East); *Saturday Night Fever The Musical* (no. 1 UK tour/Theatre Royal Bath/English Theatre Frankfurt); *Aladdin* (Roses Theatre); *The Tailor Made Man* (Charing Cross Theatre); *Under a Foreign Sky* (Theatre Centre); *The Fumidor* (Pants on Fire Theatre Company). Film and television work includes: *Parc Glan Gwil* (series regular);

UNCLE, *Mudtown* (Severn Screen/Bad Wolf); *Hollyoaks* (Channel 4); *Dal Y Mellt* (Netflix/Vox Pictures); *Age of Outrage* (BBC Wales); *Cymry Feiral*, *Cymry Feiral yn Glits I Gyd*, *O'r Diwedd*, *Pobol y Cwm*, *Rownd a Rownd*, *Merched Parchus*, *Hansh* (S4C); *Flick* (American Films).

—

WRITER – Luke Hereford *(they/them)*, as a writer Luke's autobiographical cabaret play *Grandmother's Closet* received critical acclaim and a sold out run at Wales Millennium Centre in 2022, before transferring to Summerhall for Edinburgh Festival Fringe and an international engagement at Det Andre Teateret in Oslo, Norway. In 2024 they co-wrote *Polly & Esther* as their drag persona Esther Parade, alongside performing partner and professional bestie Polly Amorous. As a theatremaker they have worked with Sherman Theatre, Cardiff, Tron Theatre, Glasgow, Royal Welsh College of Music and Drama, National Theatre Wales and Lincoln Center Theater in New York City.

DIRECTOR – Izzy Rabey *(she/they)*, is a director, facilitator and music maker from Machynlleth in mid-Wales. Izzy was the first Welsh trainee director at The Royal Court Theatre (2020–21), and an associate artist at Pentabus Theatre Company (2021–22). In 2023 Izzy won the Selar Award for Contributions to Welsh Arts and Cultural Activism. Izzy has directed work for the Royal Court, the Southbank Centre, National Theatre Wales, The Pleasance, Kiln Theatre, English Touring Theatre Company, among others. Izzy has toured work to the USA, Hawaii, Brazil, Kenya and New Zealand, and is a module leader on the MA in Queer Performance at Rose Bruford College. She is currently working on projects at Kiln Theatre, the Southbank Centre, Theatre Deli and on a short film with GobbyGirl Productions.

DESIGNER – Cara Evans *(they/she)*, is a London based performance designer. Cara graduated in Design for Stage from the Royal Central School of Speech and Drama and was a reader at the Royal Court. Theatre work includes: as designer or co-designer, *Sleepova* (Bush Theatre); *Dear Young Monster* (Bristol Old Vic and Soho); *Dynolwaith* (Sherman); *The Living Newspaper* (Royal Court); *Ugly Sisters* (Soho and New Diorama); *Wish You Were Here* (Gate Theatre); *Get Dressed!* (Unicorn); *Feral Monster* (National Theatre Wales); *Statues* (Bush Theatre); *Queer Upstairs* (Royal Court); *Body Show* (Soho Theatre); *Educating Rita* (Reading REP); *Sylvia* (English Theatre Frankfurt); *It's a Motherf**king Pleasure* (international tour); *Millennium Girls* (Brixton House); *The Maladies* (KILN); *Sirens* (Mercury Colchester); *SK Shlomo: Breathe* (Royal Albert Hall); *F**king Men* (Waterloo East); *The Beach House* (Park Theatre); *GRILLS* (CPT); *Love Bomb* (National Youth Theatre); *Baba Joon* (Swansea Grand Studio); *Bright Half Life* (King's Head); *The Misandrist* (Arcola); *Instructions for a Teenage Armageddon* (Southwark Playhouse); as associate designer for Chloe Lamford, *Teenage Dick* (Donmar Schools' Tour).

LIGHTING DESIGNER – Marty Langthorne *(he/him);* is an artist and lighting designer whose work encompasses live art, theatre, dance and fine art. Recent credits include: *Feral Monster* (National Theatre of Wales); *Zoetrope & Mabon* (National Dance Company of Wales); *Showmanism* by Dickie Beau (Hampstead Theatre); *My English Persian Kitchen* (Soho Theatre); *It's Come to This* by Meow Meow (Soho Theatre); *When The World Turns* (Oily Cart); *Wild Mix* by Jenny Moore (Southbank Centre). He is co-creator of First Light, an immersive installation of light and sound for babies. As part of the Duckie Collective, he has designed many of their theatrical club events. As a light artist he creates installations investigating human response to colour in the natural world.

SOUND DESIGNER – Barbs Dudek *(they/she),* is a contemporary music composer and a singer-songwriter, who lives and works in London. A native of Poland, their interests oscillate between electroacoustic and vocal music often queering traditional conventions. Her writing encapsulates solo, chamber, choral and orchestral pieces with frequent use of electronics. A Trinity Laban's alumnus their music has been broadcast by BBC Radio 3 and BBC 6 and on screen at BFI and the Short Film Corner at Cannes. Barbara often collaborates internationally; the latest include a Welsh-Sorbian project in Kufa Hoyerswerda 2025 and an animation *The Spirit of Ukraine* in addition to their ongoing relationship with Vox Urbane.

INTIMACY COORDINATOR – Emma Weissensteiner *(she/her)*, is an intimacy director/coordinator and choreographer working across stage and screen industries. A graduate of Central School of Ballet, Emma had an extensive career as a dancer before transitioning into intimacy direction and choreography for theatre, opera, dance, film and TV. Recent Intimacy and Choreography work includes, *Jesus Christ Superstar* (Watermill Theatre); *Cyrano de Bergerac* (Oxford University); *This City is Ours* (BBC); *Finding Father Christmas* (Channel 4); *Outlander Blood of My Blood* (Starz/MGM); *Emmerdale* (ITV); *The Hairdresser Mysteries* (BBC); *Coronation Street* (ITV); *G'wed* (ITV); *The Cleaner* (BBC); *Hollyoaks* (Channel 4). Recently Emma was recognised as a Broadcast Hot Shot for 2025 for her dedication and rising profile in the industry as an intimacy coordinator.

STAGE MANAGER – Maia Thompson (she/her) is a stage manager based in London. Originally from the US, she recently graduated from the Production and Technical Arts program at the London Academy of Music and Dramatic Art. She has worked as a member of the stage management team on various productions including *Wendy & Peter* (Watermill Theatre); *Snow White* (Eden Court Theatre); *The Maids* (Jermyn Street Theatre); *The 25th Annual Putnam County Spelling Bee* (Edinburgh Fringe). Maia also has a BFA in Film Production from Emerson College in Boston.

ASSISTANT DIRECTOR – Eugenia Taylor *(they/them)*, is a queer multidisciplinary artist and facilitator based in Cardiff, working across theatre, movement, socially-engaged arts and film. Their practice centres on co-creation, care and community, with a focus on amplifying underrepresented voices. Eugenia joined Common/Wealth Theatre in 2025 as a creative youth producer/facilitator and community cast co-ordinator on *Demand the Impossible*. They have delivered projects with Rubicon Dance, Oasis Cardiff, Parc Arts, Hijinx Theatre, House of Deviant, The Talent Shack and schools across South Wales. As a filmmaker, they have created two short films; *We Are the Pulse* and the stop-motion animation *Longing*, which was selected from hundreds of submissions to be exhibited at Tŷ Pawb.

PORTER'S CARDIFF

Porter's is a bar, music venue, and theatre – and so much more. Since opening our doors in 2012, we've grown into a buzzing three-storey hangout for live music fans, theatre-goers, art lovers, and anyone who enjoys a night out that's a bit unusual.

We're community-led and run on collaboration, believing in a safe, welcoming space where people can be themselves, connect, and create. Our calendar is shaped by the people who use it; from gigs, theatre, and open mics to board games, socials, panel talks, and workshops with industry experts from all creative fields.

Whether you're here to put on a show, discover something new, or just have a pint and a chat with pals, you'll find a warm welcome and plenty going on.

Porter's exists as a 'blank canvas' that provides opportunities for creatives to showcase their original work, and a launch pad for people starting out on their creative journeys. We do this by providing an accessible and malleable space for ideas, events, and opportunities for the community. We believe in the power art has to empower and connect a community, and by supporting artists and audiences, we help keep culture alive, authentic, and accessible to all.

Porter's is a home for creatives, a place where ideas can grow with the support that they need to thrive.

Porter's Theatre is run by:

Alice Rush (she/her)

Alice is a disabled theatre maker, producer and programmer who, along with Frankie, was some of the first drama students to step through Porter's doors back in 2012. Since then she's dreamed of running a fringe venue in Cardiff and now she does – yay! Previously she's worked with National Theatre Wales/TEAM Collective Cymru, Chapter Arts

Centre, Arch 468 and Rose Theatre Kingston. She particularly loves autobiographical weird work, especially when alcohol consumption is not only encouraged but actively facilitated.

Frankie-Rose Taylor (she/her)

Frankie is a theatre maker, producer, and Cardiff's favourite cockney. She is passionate about platforming emerging artists and theatre that is a bit weird and different – so getting to run her own venue with her best mate Alice in the dirty basement of her favourite bar is a dream come true. Frankie has spent the last ten years working across the arts in various roles – from West End theatre marketing, to feminist circus administrating, to most recently producing and programming Wales Millennium Centre's Cabaret venue. She also makes her own DIY, autobiographical, pint-fuelled shows as CB4 Theatre with Alice and pals Luke and Em.

Dan Porter (he/him)

After a twelve-year stint failing as a professional actor, Dan founded Porter's in 2012. Porter's was imagined as a place for good people to have good times, with a focus on the arts and entertainment, and with a desire to support talent on its way to bigger and better things. With Porter's Theatre, Dan is particularly interested in connecting and crossing over the theatre makers and music makers of Cardiff and Wales, and doing the same for their respective audiences. He is also always interested in connecting with people with more sense than money, and those with more money than sense.

This version of NICE THINGS: A QUEER LOVE STORY was performed at the Pleasance Theatre Islington from 1–4 April 2026.

www.pleasance.co.uk

PLEASANCE THEATRE TRUST

The Pleasance has been at the heart of Fringe theatre and comedy since 1985. With an international profile and a network of alumni that reads like a Who's Who of contemporary comedy, drama and entertainment, the Pleasance is a place for the experimental and the new.

The Pleasance is both a Festival Organisation of 27 temporary venues across three sites, and a London theatre and development centre, with two permanent performance spaces which operate year-round. The Pleasance in London and Edinburgh are entirely symbiotic. We're been a registered charity since 1995 in England and Wales and 2012 in Scotland, supporting opportunities for artists year round.

Anthony Alderson
DIRECTOR

Martyn Wood
HEAD OF OPERATIONS

Ellie Simpson
HEAD OF THEATRE LONDON

Ryan Taylor
HEAD OF COMEDY

Jonny Patton
HEAD OF THEATRE EDINBURGH

Natalie Denton
DEVELOPMENT PRODUCER

Janine Stolz
HEAD OF FINANCE

Ella Carmen Dale
DEVELOPMENT PRODUCER (MATERNITY COVER)

Charlotte McShane
OPERATIONS COORDINATOR

Stuart Hurford
HEAD OF MARKETING

Alice Gorman
DESIGNER

Nell Dobson
SOCIAL MEDIA ASSISTANT

Emma Corley
DEPUTY BOX OFFICE MANAGER

Georgie Franklin
BOX OFFICE MANAGER

Dave Burn
LONDON TECHNICAL MANAGER

Helen Duda
SENIOR VENUE TECHNICIAN

Tom Heath
FINANCE COORDINATOR

Nic Watson
EDINBURGH TECHNICAL MANAGER

Ana Webb-Sanchez
TECHNICIAN

Nice Things:
A Queer Love Story

Characters

He, *cis gay male*
They, *AMAB non-binary*

Both in their late twenties / early thirties

Interruptions

Loads of interruption; the point where one character interrupts the other is signified by '/' in the point of conversation. Their interruption is marked by '//'.

These really *are just guidelines. As long as in those lines there is some kind of stumble and interruption between the two characters, if the actors would rather find their own rhythm, that's encouraged, if not, preferable. Just make sure the full lines are said, unless specified.*

After and Before

The scenes are all moments after or before They comes out to He as non-binary. The distance between that event is given in the script but this is just a guide, and these specifics probably shouldn't be given to the audience. However there should be signifiers in the environment to signify the audience which scenes are **BEFORE** *and which are* **AFTER**. *Lighting, movement, sound, projection, whatever that is.*

* * * * * *within scenes indicates a small passing of time from one moment to the next. It could be a few minutes, a few hours, probably never more than that.*

References

There are references throughout the script to Cardiff, and locations within the city but the play can be set anywhere really. Change these references accordingly. Ideally it should be a city with a relatively small LGBTQ+ scene. It's probably not London or Manchester.

They's Dance

I've been specifically non-specific about what song this is. It feels like it should come from the actor, or at least the rehearsal process so that it's something kind of relevant to the queer community at the time in which the production is being made. Not necessarily by a queer artist though.

Special thanks to François Pandolfo, Elliot Ditton, Twm Bollen-Molloy, Erwan Sion and Joel Dafydd for reading the sketchy early drafts, Kate Wasserberg and Davina Moss for being great dramaturgical friends, Matthew Xia, James Ley, Sparrow Coffee Shop for the space to furiously write and rewrite – drafts, funding applications et al. – Alice, Frankie and Dan at Porter's, Royal Welsh College of Music and Drama, Michael and Connor for always being pals, Phil Jones and the unstoppable Philippa Mannion and Josh and Winnie for being the best family I could have ever wished for.

And finally, to Izzy Rabey for having faith from day one.

For all the hairy enbies, who owe *nobody* androgyny

Ten Seconds After

He Right.

Okay.

They Yeah?

He What?

They What?

He I –

Really?

They Yes.

He Right.

Okay.

They Okay, as / in, you're okay with it?

He // Oh well, it doesn't really –

Well, yeah of course.

I'm –

They Okay

He I mean it *is* a bit . . .

Of a . . .

Change?

They Yes.

He And I think it *is* maybe a bit weird for / me . . .

They // Weird?

He I just mean that it's definitely going / to take some . . .

They // No, no, I understand / that, and I

He // So, how did you know?

Like, when did you –

They A while?

He Okay.

They A while, yeah.

I'm sorry that I didn't tell you / before.

He // No, *no*, I'm not trying to –

It's fine, of course it's fine.

They It is?

He I mean it's fine that you didn't tell me until you were ready to –

They Oh, right, yeah. Yeah.

He And the rest of it, is, too. Obviously.

They Yeah?

He Yeah.

Yes. It has to be. So, it will be.

Three Months Before

He It isn't working. The rest of the room is, like . . . away. Pointing away. It's –

They I like it.

He Okay, but it just doesn't . . . w –

They It works for me.

He No.

They Wow.

Okay, so what should / we do?

He // It's wrong. It's wrong.

It's wrong, babe. It just, it. It. It.

Is.

Sorry, I'm sorry, you know how I can get about these sorts of . . . I just want it to be perfect, because it –

They No, no no no no no, don't be sorry it's fine, we're going to fix it, together!

He Okay.

They Yeah?

He Okay, okay.

They How do we fix it then?

He We need an angel.

They Huh?

He An angel. For the, the –

They Why do we / need . . . I don't –

He // Or a star? We need a star or an angel for the top.

They Okay. Why?

He It's traditional. A star or an angel is traditional.

They Well, we're not traditional.

Are we?

He Babe, please, this is the first time ever that I've hosted –

That / we've . . .

They // Okay okay okay, listen, it's fine. I'll go to John Lewis, tomorrow, when you're in work –

He Yeah?

They – and I'll find us a lovely star or an angel, for the top.

And then we'll have the perfect Christmas tree.

* * * * *

They Okay, so I didn't get an angel / or a star.

He // Oh my god, no why?

They But, *but,* I got us something else! Something else for the top of the tree . . .

He Oh. You did?

They I think you'll like it.

He Show me, show me!

They *reveals a hand crafted Christmas tree topper, with the faces of the four Golden Girls.*

He It's –

They The Golden Girls!

He It's The Golden Girls.

They You love The Golden Girls.

He Well, I've not really / watched it since –

They // For the top of the tree!

He The Golden Girls on the top of our tree?

They Yes. They're angels *and* stars.

He The Golden Girls are angels and stars?

They Well, they were all movie stars, and . . . they're all dead.

He Yeah, I got it.

They Though, I guess, Bea Arthur was more of a Broadway star . . .

He I guess she was.

They Do you like it?!

He Yes.

They Are you sure?

He Well, I'd have been happy with the angel, / but, I suppose –

They // But this is a bit more fun, isn't it? A bit more . . .

Us.

Don't you think?

He A bit more you, maybe.

They Oh come on! You *love* The Golden Girls too!

He No I know . . . it's just

Actually, it's nothing. I love it. I think they'll look perfect on the top.

They And you *love* me

He I suppose.

They You're *such* a Dorothy.

Fifteen Minutes After

He What is it, babe?

They Nothing.

He Are you disappointed that you didn't have like . . . this *dramatic* coming out?

They Fuck off, no.

He No? Not even / a bit?

They // Fuck off.

He Hey, I'm teasing!

They I just thought you'd have questions.

He I do, yeah. Loads.

They Okay.

Okay then.

Do you want to ask

Me?

He Okay. As long as you're –

They Yeah, I'm fine, just ask me.

He Okay, I guess I was wondering about . . . hair.

They What about it?

He What are you going to do with it?

They Same as I always do, I think?

He No, I mean like . . . you're hairy, right, which isn't very . . . is it?

They Oh come on –

He Well, I'm just asking! I've never seen –

Not with, like, facial or or or a hairy chest, or . . .

What's wrong, am I / saying the wrong –

They // Okay, no, listen: I think, I *think,* the hair stays? Okay?

He So you're saying, you're not necessarily a boy, but you'll still be

Still look like –

They Yes, I said I'm not necessarily a boy, but also, I'm not necessarily *not* a boy.

So I can do what I want with, with . . . hair. That makes sense, doesn't it?

He No.

Sorry, babe.

They Jesus, I –

He Hey, don't / get –

They // I'm not getting –

He It's fine, it is! Of course it is!

But – just – you wanted me to / ask questions –

They // Well, you've started off great!

He Hey!

They Okay, sorry. Sorry. You're right.

What else?

He Do you think it will change how we fuck?

They What?

He Sex, the way we, have –

They No.

He No?

They No, not at all, no.

He But what if, like, in sex, you know sometimes you like me to call you things . . .

They Yeah.

He Like, you know, like good boy, / like daddy, that stuff?

They // I haven't really thought –

He Oh.

Okay.

They Okay?

He Well, I thought you would have, before telling me?

They Not in terms of / sex, no, I think, it –

He // Okay, so, then in what terms *have* you thought about it?

They I don't know / why you're –

He // Have you thought about it at all?

They Can you / just –

He // Because if you haven't thought about it at all and you're just gonna, like, what, spring this on / me, I'm gonna have these questions and I want you –

They // Spring this on you, like it . . . yeah, right, I asked for them.

He So have you thought about this? Are you sure this is right?

They Why do you say it like it's a decision, like, what answer I'm gonna give in a pub quiz?

He A pub quiz? What?

They Yeah . . . I don't fucking know! Like I'm being, fickle, or –

He Babe, I just want to know how it's going to change us.

They It isn't.

He Right.

They At all.

He And you're still . . .

Are you still

Gay?

Are you not . . .

Not gay? Anymore?

They Yes.

He Yes what?

They Yes, I'm gay.

He Okay.

That is . . . yeah that *is* a little confusing to me.

They Why?

He Because you've just told me you're not a boy?

They Oh jesus, / it isn't so –

He // But being gay, means, boys who like / boys, doesn't it?

They // Will you just –

He But if you're not a boy how can you

Still be . . . ?

Sorry, but I don't think I get it. This side of it, I don't. No. I don't get it.

They Well, if you let me –

He Okay.

They I guess

I see

Gay

As the sex. The sexuality. My sexuality?

He Yes. Yes, I understand that.

They Obviously.

But I don't see it as –

Like, that's just . . . sex.

He Oh, so I'm just . . . oh my / god –

They // Oh, fuck, fuck, no. I mean, that's just the part of *me* that has sex.

Sexuality.

Right? Right, right, right?

He Right!

They Right! Which is different to

I mean that, for me, being queer is more than just the me that has sex, yeah? I'm queer in every part of my, like –

Everything. Clothes, films, TV, music, the way that I / want to present –

He // I know that . . .

They Exactly! You know that. So you know that

In the world, I don't feel that I fit in with . . .

With –

He Boy?

They Exactly! Yes.

He I think

I – I'm just trying / to figure . . .

They // I know –

He No, no you don't know. Actually.

Because you've just

All *you've* had to do is say these . . . words. Words. Like, it's just. Words.

Words.

They Exactly. It *is* just words. So why are you getting –

He I'm not, getting –

They Yes you are. You're uncomfortable.

He I'm not uncomfortable, I'm / confused!

They // It's nothing to get uncomfortable about.

Like you said, it's just words. It's just two words. Two words.

He Well yeah, that's part of the problem if I'm honest, babe.

They What?

He Like, like, there's not even a

Not actually, even a

It's not even fucking – it doesn't seem fucking . . . real?

It's this

Two hyphenated words. There isn't even like a proper – proper

Word, you've just had to put two words together to make up this

This –

They Huh.

Hah.

He What?

They I just really, *really* did not expect you to respond this way.

He This way? What –

They You think I've made this up.

He I never said *you've* made it up, / I just . . .

They // I just don't know why you're being so

So

Two Months Before

They Extravagant.

He I know. Do you like it?

They I –

He It really suits you.

They Yeah?

He Really. Really sexy.

They Yeah.

He I might actually rip it off.

They Oop, don't rip it, please.

How much was it?

He A lot.

They A lot?

He Yeah. Two hundred.

They Two hundred?!

He Well, two fifty, really –

They Two fifty?! Oh my god.

He Yeah, that packaging and –

They Jesus Christ.

He Happy Birthday!

They What?

He No, not you. Happy Birthday to / Jesus Christ.

They // Jesus.

He Because you said / Jesus Christ.

They // Jesus Christ.

Two hundred and fifty?

He Including postage.

They Yeah.

He And packaging.

They Yep.

Right.

Thank you.

But –

He But?

They I'm not sure if I like it.

He Oh.

They No. It's a bit –

He Because I really like it / on you.

They // I know you do.

He Yeah, it's really nice.

They It's nice. It is.

He Yeah?

They Yeah. It's really nice.

He It is?

They Yeah. It's lovely. It *is* –

He So you do like it?

They No.

He What? I thought it was really nice. It's a nice

Isn't it?

They It is nice.

He It is? Great! Great, babe. Great!

They Objectively.

He Objecti –

Shit, shit. Fuck! I thought you'd love it, I thought it was the / perfect –

They // It's not. But that's only because I don't like it on me

It just – it just isn't me.

You like it, because

Because –

He Because?

They It just isn't me.

* * * * *

He You really don't need to / feel embarrassed.

They // I do, though.

He I like them! Both of them.

They But see, this is it. *Both*. Only *both*.

He I said, before, that it's absolutely fine.

They But it *does* feel like I didn't get you enough.

He Well that's just you being / silly.

They // No, not me being silly.

You got me *so much*.

He I know.

They Which actually felt a bit weird.

He What? Weird?

They Well like, I had to stand there and open, what, fifteen, sixteen presents, and all of them pretty, none of them, really, were like cheap, silly / things from –

He // No, a few of them were –

They Well, even so, just me opening all those gifts in front of your family and / I never got to –

He // My family? I don't know why my –

They No, it's not about them. I just felt. Opening them all in front of them, I felt –

He Embarrassed?

They Yes.

He Weird?

They A bit yeah. It was a bit / weird.

He // So now getting you gifts is –

They Well, it was just a lot of stuff.

He Stuff?

They Yeah, well no not *stuff*. Not like, in a mean way, not like . . . '*from a pile of stuff*'

He –

They Devil Wears Prada.

He Right.

They Yeah.

He I just like buying you things. It's not that deep.

They Okay.

He Is it okay?

They It makes me feel a bit small.

He Oh come on.

They You know I will never be able to –

He I don't care. I do not care. I don't do it so that you can, like, match me. It isn't about that. Nothing like that. I just want you to have nice things. And I can afford to buy you nice things. So why can't I buy you nice things?

Do you want me to stop buying you nice things?

Do you actually not want the nice things? Because I can stop. And I can return all the presents.

If you want? Do you want me to do that?

They Not particularly.

He Thought not.

They I just wish I could –

He Don't even say it!

They – repay you!

I do!

He Well, I get to sleep next to you, every night

So, I think that's a pretty fair deal.

Don't you?

They It could be worse for you couldn't it?

He Much worse.

They Do we have any more Ferrero Rocher?

Twenty-Five Minutes After

He I promise, I'm not trying to be –

They No, I know,

He This is a change for me. Too. It's a change for both of us. For us. Our. Us.

They You're right.

I know.

And I know you're not going to be . . .

He No.

They Right away.

He But I'll try.

They Okay.

He Okay.

Except.

I'm still . . .

Not entirely –

Nothing is actually changing about you, is it?

They Well –

He It's just, really, babe, really;

He, him, they, them, him, they, he, us, you, I / don't know –

They // How do you keep getting this so wrong?

He – What difference does it actually make?

They Well to me, it –

I don't really want to define, or

Identify. With –

He Wait, wait. So, wait. You don't *want* to.

They I –

He You *can*, but you won't because –

They I don't –

He You don't want to.

Fuck, that is really

It's kind of selfish and a bit fucked up. Actually, yeah . . . it's / really

fucked up, you know?

They // Jesus Christ.

He Babe, I'm sorry, I'm sorry that I can't just be okay with this like straight away, because I really wish I could but you're my

You're my

And you don't

And it doesn't actually change *anything* about you other than

You're just saying that you no longer

That you don't want to

As if being a man isn't good enough for you? Like it doesn't actually

Like you can be something more, more

Better. More, controversial, more

They More?

He It's always a statement. With you

You have to put your fucking middle finger up to anything that means you might be any stretch or thread of

Just *anything* close to. To.

They Say it.

He Normal.

You just can't stand being normal.

Ten Days Before

He Oh my god!

They Yeah?

He Yeah. Fuck yeah.

They Yeah?

He Yeah?

They Oh –

He What?

They I

Ew. Ugh. Hair in my / mouth.

He // Hair? Oh, gross.

They Yeah, but it's like, not

Pah, pah, pah, PAH

He Not what? Babe?

They Yeah, it's like from the fucking throw or / something.

He // Oh gross.

They Yeah.

Ack. Aaaaaaaaaaaaaaaack.

He Wait, why don't –

They No, I don't want to stop!

Haaaaaaaagggggggghhhhh.

Haaagh. Haaagh. Haaagh. Hagh. Hagh.

Okay I'm good.

He You're so sexy baby

They Yeah?

He Yeah, so fucking sexy

They Call me baby

He You're so sexy baby, you're my fucking / sexy baby boy

They // Yeah. Yeah

Oh, no not that

He What?

They Not baby boy, not baby *boy*

He Sorry okay

They Call me something else

He You're my

Beautiful little

Slut!

* * * * *

They It's always good.

He So fucking good!

They Thank god we're sexually compatible.

He Yeah.

It was different today.

They Yeah?

He Yeah. A bit.

They Good, different?

He Yeah. I think so, yeah. Always good.

They I liked it.

He I know you did.

They I really liked it when you called me names.

He Not all of them though . . .

Right?

They Maybe just not 'baby boy'.

He No?

They No. It's like

Too infantilising?

He But 'baby' is okay?

They Yeah.

He Just not 'baby boy?'

They No, it makes it sound like 'a' baby boy. You know. Infantilised. Not the same.

He Okay, not baby boy.

They No.

He Fine.

They Thank you.

Hey, next time

Can you call me princess?

He Really?

They Yes.

He You'd really like that?

They I don't know. Until I try, really.

He Sure.

They Yeah?

He Sure. Princess.

Thirty Minutes After

He I wish this was easier / for

They // It's easier for you than it is for me, I promise

He Babe, I know –

They I wish you could see it from my perspective

And then you'd see I'm not saying this just to, to make some point.

It's just, finally I have words to

A way to

Understand.

He I know.

I'm sorry. I'll try to listen.

And – and, understand, and –

They Please do.

He Okay.

But still, I might need time to –

They Oh my / fucking god

He // Just a *bit,* a bit, to adjust and get used to

The changes

The new

New pronouns and stuff

You might just have to be patient with me.

Please.

Babe?

They Okay.

He Okay.

I love you.

It's going to be fine.

Two Days Before

They It was euphoric!

He Canal Street?

They Yeah.

He Was euphoric?

They Don't take the piss!

He I'm not, you're cute.

They Thanks. But it *was* euphoric. That weekend, it really was.

He Okay.

They So: It was a month, maybe, before I met you.

The first time I'd ever gone out in a skirt –

He You went out in a skirt?

They Yeah. And –

He What kind of skirt?

They Like a black, black and white plaid skirt. Very . . . The Craft?

He Okay.

They And everyone was like getting down and dirty to Rhianna or whatever, and

I was like

Really

He Really?

They Really nervous? Nervous to go to Manchester with them all. Wasn't sure if I fitted in with them, really.

He Your friends?

They Yeah. Or if I would fit in with – Manchester, I guess? But before I went, Connor was like, 'Just go for yourself, babe, don't worry about all that friends fitting in bollocks, just go for yourself.'

He He was with you?

They No, no he didn't go. So all weekend I just had this voice in my head like 'Go for yourself, babe, just go for yourself, do it for yourself . . . '

Like a gay, Welsh . . . Jiminy Cricket, Fairy Godmother, you know? So I did.

He Did what?

They Go for myself. Forgot all the friends bollocks. I did it for myself. And they were all getting wrecked, dancing, having a blast, and so was I, but I wasn't With them? I was like, somewhere else? Having a totally different experience.

He Euphoric.

They Exactly. So I just stepped out onto the cobbles, and there was

This . . . joy. And I just fucking cried. In a fucking skirt. And with my eyeliner, and my pink hair, remember my pink hair?

He Mm hm.

They Yeah. And I cried. On the cobbles, this euphoric, overwhelming moment on the cobbles. Like, Deirdre fucking Barlow.

And then this beautiful, beautiful guy came over to me and asked me if I was okay, and I was like. Yeah. I'm great. And we kissed. And it was like the best kiss I'd ever ever had, because –

He Woah woah woah woah

They No, not the best, I'd ever, I mean / it was but up until that point

He // Yeah yeah, right, steady on

They I guess what I mean is it was

It was / different.

He // Yeah, different, okay

They You're not

It was different because he was trans.

He Oh. Okay.

They He saw my nails, I'd done the trans flag colours on my nails.

And he was like, oh your nails are the trans flag. And I was like, yeah, and he was like, I'm trans.

He Okay.

What do you want me to

They Nothing

Nothing at all, I just

It was part of my weekend in Manchester, with

My, my, my, my –

He Euphoric?

They Yes! My euphoric weekend in Manchester!

When I wore a skirt, and had painted nails and eyeliner and kissed a trans guy and felt –

He Euphoric?

They Yes!

He I do have a question.

Do you find trans guys attractive?

They I guess it depends on the guy?

That's like asking if you find all cis gay guys attractive? A trans guy is just a guy.

He Right.

But –

They But?

He Well, I'm just curious to know if

Like, it's great that you kissed this guy and it was amazing and

I think you

But what if you wanted to. To –

They To?

He Well, I'm just thinking like –

They He was just a beautiful, / man, and we –

He // Did he have a dick?

They Does that matter?

He I

No. Of course not.

To him

They But it does to you?

He No! No, no, no, no. I'm not saying

What I am

I mean, it would have mattered to you / if you had

They // No, it definitely wouldn't have, in any –

He Yes, it would, babe. If you had hooked up with this guy. Of course you

Like

If he didn't have a dick, then

Would you find that

Would you be able to

Or even *want* to

They I don't know.

But either way, he was a beautiful guy. So handsome. And we had this incredible moment. That was all.

He Can I just –

They Yes?

He Why are you telling me this?

Do you want to try / and have

They // No, no! Of course not, I'm with you, we're –

He Well, at the time did you

Were you interested in it / going further?

They // I don't know!

I'm just sharing a moment of

A moment where I felt, in that moment that I could have

O, *god,* I dunno! It just felt

He Euphoric?

A Week After

They Can I give you an example?

He Of?

They An example. A, like . . . tangible example of how it feels.

For me.

He Yes, please.

Please. I want to –

They Okay.

I always used to find it weird when a mum would come into the shop. Like mums with their kids?

He Right, yeah.

They Yeah, like in the shop. So they'd be walking around with their kids, letting them pick things up, smell things. Like the kid was doing the shopping. Like the mother was giving them a sort of grown up experience. Letting the kid shop. You know? And then they'd choose their soap or their lip balm or whatever and they'd get to the till – even if it wasn't actually for the kid – there'd be this little transaction where the kid would pay.

He The kid would pay?

They No. Yeah, but not like, *pay*. Like the mum would give the kid the money and the kid would want to pay. Like a grown up, or whatever. Like the kid was a grown up, doing a grown up thing and buying a bar of soap. And the mum would always say: 'Give the money to the man.'

Just: 'Give the money to the man.'

And I always found that, really . . . like, cringe? Cringey?

He Right, I see

They And I used to think it was because I was like seventeen. Seventeen, eighteen. So I wasn't a man.

He Yet.

They Yeah, exactly, yet.

But to this kid who wanted this like, grown up experience of shopping, paying for a soap, or whatever, I was 'the man'.

Just, the man who worked in the shop. Like I was a man. Even though I never felt like a man. To this child, I was the man who sold them the soap.

He Yeah.

They But I wasn't. A man. So it always felt . . .

He Felt?

They Wrong.

He I can see that.

They Yeah?

He Yeah. You were a baby.

They No, that isn't

Well, yeah, I was. But now I realise it's because it –

He Wasn't true?

They Right! Exactly!

He Right.

But, it is?

Kind of?

They No, it isn't

He But you said to me you didn't necessarily / identify as

They // Not necessarily, no.

He So that means that sometimes you feel like you *are* a man, right?

They No, you're not listening.

He Yes I am. And to this, mum, kid, strangers, whatever, you *are* a man.

They But I'm not.

He Babe, you are always going to, how do you, what do you say?

They Present?

He Present, yes, present like a man. You just

I'm not saying it's right, but, that is what the world sees you as.

You can't get pissed off when like . . . people, normal, strangers, or whoever call you a man. Or, like 'sir' or, whatever, because you just

You look like a guy, babe. You do.

They But what does that mean?

He Just a guy.

Whatever we've been told to think a guy is, or

Looks like

So as long as you look like this, and you're not planning on changing how you . . . are you?

They No.

He No, so as long as you look like this, people are going to assume that

Aren't they?

They I just wish they didn't.

He I know.

I'm sorry, babe.

They It's not your

But I do think that some people have realised –

He What do you mean?

They I don't think I was the first to know.

You remember when I told you about, in school. My music exam?

He Singing?

They 'SHOULD HAVE SUNG A BOYS SONG' in red ink, like teacher's congealed blood. But my music teacher was like . . . a proper ally. And she fought it. She fought that external examiner, whatever and

She was actually the one who encouraged me to sing that song

To sing 'Somewhere That's Green'; cause when we did Little Shop, and I was like Year 9, Year 10, we had this whole conversation about how she thinks Audrey would be great played by a boy. That I would have been

And I think that she maybe saw in me that I was

Wasn't

You see what I mean, don't you?

He Well . . .

They Well?

He Okay. It's

I get it. She recognised something in you. By saying that. By seeing something

And seeing how you didn't fit

But I also . . . I . . . I / never fitted in with the boys. Like on the fucking rugby tour to fucking, fucking, Vienna or whatever.

They // This isn't

He But, I just didn't

It doesn't mean that I couldn't *be* a boy. Like, I am, I have

I have a

How does it work? Does it work this way where I can just . . . choose? Like, I can't just choose another way to be.

Can I?

Can you?

They Oh *my* god.

He No, please listen, I'm not trying to be

I'm just saying making that choice so

So

Abruptly? It's going to take some time to

Because it doesn't just affect / you, does it?

They // Oh my fucking / god

He // Babe, I'm not trying / to

They // Yes, you are trying, to to –

He I'm just saying it's a big change for other people, not / just you

They // Well, that sounds like a them problem

He Don't be, please don't that's so selfish and ridiculous, / you know you're not the only person in the world. Not everything has to be

They // Ridiculous? Wow, I didn't know that being honest with myself was ridiculous, now, is it? Ridiculous? / Jesus fucking . . .

He // But you've always been –

Okay, here, here is what what I can't get my head around. It's that you've always been

And now you've just – or it's, it seems like you have

Decided

They No. It doesn't / work like that

He // Then tell me, babe. Please tell me how it *does* work.

Because from where

I'm

From where I'm standing last week you were my boyfriend and now you're

So it is. You *have*

Decided. Surely I'm not being – narrow, small, closed, narrow – whatever, when I say that you *have* decided that you don't want to use –

They It isn't a *decision*. Did you *decide* to be gay? Was it a decision?

He A bit actually

Yeah, I think it was a decision, a bit.

They I can't –

He Yes, I decided that I wanted to

Pursue it.

They Wow –

He You're doing it now. The thing where I speak and it isn't. Isn't

Right. For you. The *right* thing to say. For you and all your . . . your friends. You all think that I always say the wrong thing. But you know what that does? It's like you think

You, not just you, you and your friends, and the, fuck, the fucking whole world, it feels like, you don't think my way of being gay is valid. Like I am invalid. My way isn't

I'm not aware enough of how to be or what to do or say or feel without I don't know the *correct* thing to say without offending someone. So then I'm always corrected and repri-

But actually, to be honest, actually, with your friends, it's just pretty much totally unavoidable. Because everything, *everything* is wrong. Offensive. To say. Everything. I can't say anything, feel, without there being some Instagram self help

Thing

That tells me, and you, and your friends, and the whole world why what I said is, or could be perceived as a . . . like, a whatever. But like. Fuck that. No, fuck that. I'm a fucking good person. I am not a bad person. And yeah, okay, I don't, what's the word you always

The, that, the, the, the, the

Phrase. Fuck. The way I

Present. PRESENT. The way I present to the world is not particularly

Queer. Gay, whatever, but that doesn't mean I haven't had to deal with

And I know you, you and your friends, and the whole world think I have never had to, but I have had to. I haven't, *I have not* had a fucking privileged carefree life. People *do* call me a fag. People *do* shout at me. Slurs. Whatever. In the streets, on the bus, at the co-op, when I'm not with you. And I do brush it off, and I do ignore it and I. But it does

Yeah, maybe that means I am scared to hold your hand. And maybe that's partly why I'm not like you. Like your friends. But, it doesn't mean that I'm not. Not.

Valid. The way I am. My way of. It is

Like, you, when you went to Manchester with those friends, those people, and they were just like getting down and dirty to Rihanna in a shitty club. Like, I don't know, why is that a bad thing? Why is that not

That's okay, isn't it? Why can't we just

Why can't they just

Exist?

Why does it always have to be this . . . big . . . big thing? Statement?

And if I say the wrong thing sometimes that doesn't always mean that I am

And yeah. I do think that being gay is *partly* a choice. I probably, yeah I could have done what my brothers did. Stayed at home, married a girl from high school, you know wife and fucking kids, and that, that, that, *that* life. That life, I could have done it. And I probably would have enjoyed it. Like, it would have been the easy thing to do. It would. Sometimes, I do think that. But I don't think I would have been

Would I have been

Been happy? Probably not. So I chose to be happy. I chose this. I did. To a

To a certain degree, I chose this. And you. I love you. And when you attack me for saying that this is not the right way to do be. That I say the wrong thing. Think it. It

Because I see you. I do, I see you roll your eyes. And I hear you inside your head, thinking, that I'm fucking, just, fucking, being some, some, like a stereotype that I get from my fucking homophobia, inner homophobia inside of me or whatever, but like, actually, you don't really. You don't

Be honest, do you actually, genuinely, truly, believe that? Or is it just the Instagram thing? Is it because you saw it on Instagram, and all your friends shared it, and all the gay celebrities shared it and so now you feel you have to share it, and that now that is the only way to think? Like you have to think that way. Because it makes *you* feel

Like you belong in that

Like your way of thinking is superior. More

And if you don't think that way that you're wrong, and a bad queer, a bad person. Because it doesn't always mean that.

It's like, it feels like, they're. Your friends. The world. Like they're . . . I don't know. *Policing* how you are

We are supposed to think. The right way to think. But what if that isn't always how I think? What does it mean? That I'm a shit person.

And that's

When that comes from the man that I love

Sorry.

The *person* that I love. It's horrible. It's really, really, really. Horrible. It's horrible.

They You just did it.

He What?

They You said you couldn't do it. But you just did it.

Thank you.

Two Days Before

He *and* **They** *sing a rousing rendition of 'Suddenly Seymour' from Little Shop of Horrors at a tacky gay bar karaoke night.* **He** *is Seymour and* **They** *is Audrey. It's fucking epic!!!*

Three Weeks After

He Baby!

They Yeah!

He Fuck yes!

They Fuck YES! Call me baby again!

He Fuck yeah, baby!

They Yes!

He You're so fucking sexy, baby

They Call me a bitch

He You're a sexy little fucking bitch baby

They Yeah! Call me baby

He Fuuuuuuuuck baby!

They Call me baby

He You little fucking princess

They Oh, no

He What is it, everything okay?

They Yeah, yeah yeah yeah

I just, don't call me that right now

He I thought you

They I just, no, it makes me feel like a girl

He Isn't that what you / want?

They // Not now, no, just call me baby

He Baby

They Call me your baby

He You're my baby

They Yeah, I fucking am, call me your baby boy

He Stop stop stop

I just. I just.

Sorry, I –

Two Days Before

He *and* **They** *are drunk.*

He What if we we

We, we we we we

He *giggles, loudly.*

They What? If we what? SHUSH!

He If we try it the other way?

They Nooooooooooooo I'm bad the other way and I

It's really

He No way can you be bad the other no way

NO

WAY

They But you're so good this way

He Yeah?

They Yeah, it's so good

He Yeah

They You're so fucking fucking fucking fucking sexy

He Sexy?

They Yeah!

He Me?

They Yeah you!

He A sexy fucking man

They With a sexy fucking cock

He Yeah yeah, you like it?

They Yeah

He Good, me too

They Can we do this forever?

He Fuck yeah

They Fucking beautiful

He You're beautiful

So fucking beautiful and sexy and

Fuck

They Yeah?

He Yeah, fuck I just feel so fucking good with you

They You are good with me

He Yeah?

They Yeah, and we're good together

He Yeah!

They YEAH –

He Wait wait wait

Slow slow slow slow slow

They Yeah?

He Yeah

They Oh fuck, fuck FUCK

He FUCK

They FUCK

He FUCK

They Yeah, you like that when I –

He NO

No I

I'm gonna be sick

Three Weeks After

He Baby boy.

They Thought so.

He Just a bit confusing, I think.

They Okay, yes.

He Because you told me, before, you said you didn't 'not necessarily a boy'

Like it

So when you asked me to call you that

And then you *didn't* want me to call you princess because it makes you feel like a girl, but before, you, you said

I mean isn't that what you want, to feel like a girl, sometimes?

They No, not at all, I never / said that

He // So what the fuck do you / want then?

They // It's not a black and white . . . thing. It isn't.

And sex, usually, is a very

Very

Boy thing, for me, I guess. If that makes / any . . .

He // Not really / actually, it doesn't.

They // Did you just, like, quote me?

He What?

They Not necessarily a boy. Not a boy, necessarily.

He Because that's something you said

Before.

They But like

You use it against / me, in like this, confrontational

He // I'm not, no, no no no, I'm just, just, I just need, I need

They Need?

He I'm trying / to understand

They // But why does it matter? Like the ins and outs of it?

When I'm naked, with you, and we're

And I'm being

I feel like a sexy boy

And I never feel like a sexy boy, any other time, because / I'm not, sexy, in

He // You are. You are sexy. You're / always sexy

They // No, no I'm not. I'm just not

He Babe

They I'm not

Not like you. The others. Grindr. All of that. I'm just not. And part of that is because I'm not a boy. But when I'm –

He The but

There's always a but

They Because –

He What?

They I don't know.

I want to explain it better, but –

He But?

They I don't know.

He I'm gonna have a shower.

Two Days Before

They Babe?

Babe?

Babe?

Babe?

He I don't wanna talk please just let me spew, please

They Okay

I feel bad

That like

Well I never top you, right? Like once in a blue moon.

And I put my dick in you and you threw up.

Are those two things related?

Babe?

Babe?

He I don't think so

They Okay

Because I

He Babe, please I just

It's just because I'm f-f-f-f . . .

He *vomits.*

It's just because I'm fucked babe.

They Okay.

Do you like when we go out together?

I do

I like when dance together, and forget all the

The shit that we

I like wearing fun things to Kings with you

Feeling protected by you

I feel safe going out and getting drunk in my sparkly top or whatever 'cause you're there to protect you

Me. You're there to protect me

Do you like it when I . . . when I wear my sparkly top?

Do you think I look sexy? And

Even though I'm not necessarily in my

Though I don't look very

Do you want some water?

Six Weeks After

They I don't know if I want to go . . .

He I'm not going on my own, babe!

They Great, then let's stay in!

He Babe.

They Golden Girls marathon!

He Babe.

They Desperate Housewives, then

He Babe.

Come with me. Hey, you can wear whatever you want.

They Hmmmmmmmmmmmmmmmmmmmmmmmm . . .

He What?

They Well, technically I can *always* wear whatever I want

He Yes, of course you can.

I didn't mean it like –

They Don't need your permission . . .

He Of course you don't. Babe, I never said

Of course. I just meant –

They It's not even about that to be honest, honestly, it's just that, they're your friends, and they're really . . . like

Well, I mean, they're all basically straight

He That's not true . . .

They No, but they –

He They're all gay. Literally, all gay.

They Yeah, maybe that's the problem . . .

He Babe. What's going on?

They Well

I feel like they treat me differently ever since

Like they all think it's really *cool* to have a partner of a friend who's

Like me

Like, they're all really

Like I'm novel. Fascinating.

He Oh fuck 'em babe!

They Well, I don't think that would solve anything . . .

He What I mean is

Who the fuck cares what they think, babe? You don't care what anyone thinks. And that's what I love about you, babe.

Always have.

They Where has this all come from?

He I just

I want you to come, and you can fucking rub it in their faces. Who you are. I want you to be proud of yourself. I want you to wear whatever the fuck you want to wear. In fact, I think you should make it as fucking . . . queer as you –

They What does that mean?

He You tell me! Show me, like, babe

I want you to

I need you to know that I am happy for you and this new way of

So tonight we can like, celebrate that and

Look, I know they can be toxic gay boys, sometimes, but they *are* my friends. And I fucking love you.

Both those things are true.

*****

They I just found a bit perverse, how they were all –

He Perverse?

They Yes! I found it perverse when all your cis gay male friends were coming up to

me and telling me how amazing I looked.

I'm not some . . . some fascinating, queer, creature for them to all be impressed by.

Just because I'm wearing, what, this?

Like, this isn't even that much of a

It's just like, fucking ASOS?!

He You're right. But they're –

They But actually, not even tonight. Not just tonight. Like when I wear nail varnish and it's just, you know, shit, cheap nail varnish, not even like

And everyone stops to tell me how much they love my nails. If I was a woman with this shit, cheap nail varnish they wouldn't even think to

They wouldn't even mention it. Or look at it. You know?

He They might

They I doubt it.

What?

He Babe, tonight you almost didn't go because you were worried / you'd be so different, that you wouldn't fit in, so you know that it's, that the way you dress, sometimes is, well, different.

They // And what I was worried about came –

He Was it really that bad?

They It just

The way I dress isn't for them, you know? It never is.

And their fascination of

This. Of me. Of me, being this

Being.

Thing.

They them.

He But it is.

They What?

He It is for other people. Kind of. Because, this isn't just your world.

And if you'd gone in some boring, some normal clothes, you'd complain because you weren't expressing your

But you go in your, in this, and it's

They You wanted me to dress like –

He You would have anyway, wouldn't you?

They Because this *is* how I dress!

He No, this is how you *choose* to dress.

Babe, that's a fact. because you look at your wardrobe and you choose this instead of

And tonight, you're right, of course I wanted you to

Because god knows I never want to *stop* you from

How could I when I lo –

I want us to be a united front on this whole thing.

They This whole thing?

He Yes. YES. This *is* a thing, that is happening to you, but also to everyone around you.

Including me. And I'm supposed to be your

You're supposed to

They Oh babe, wait, let's –

He Why are you so unhappy? You're unhappy with

It makes you *un*happy to

To just blend in. Dress down. But you dress up, which I want, and everyone says you look amazing and it's still, not the right reaction?

I'm trying. I'm really trying. I can't speak for everyone else, but I'm really

I really am.

They I sometimes just feel like I don't belong.

He Where?

They Here

Anywhere

He What do you mean?

You belong with me still

Don't you?

You feel like you do, don't you?

You want me to get better at all of this? You want me to keep trying?

That is what you want, isn't it?

They The music tonight was so shit.

He Babe?

They Boring. Like them.

He They're my friends.

They Yeah, but you're not boring. You're nothing like them.

We're nothing like them.

You know last time we were there, I accidentally ended up in the kitchen alone with Aled, and he spoke to me about his kitchen island for nine minutes.

Nine. Minutes.

How it took him so long to measure it all out, find the perfect colour that

would be a statement, but not too bold, not so dark that it brings the mood of the room down, could still endure cosmetic damage bla bla bla bla and my *god* it was so boring I wanted to die

In the following, **They** *puts on some music. It's something queer coded, but probably by a female artist rather than a queer one, it's got a beat and they're playing it obnoxiously loud.*

If we were ever like that, I just

Fuck, because we're not that at all. We're queer. We're fucking queer and it's amazing. And this is our queer flat. With queer art on the walls. Queer plates in the cupboard. Queer fucking films on our Netflix fucking watchlist. And this, this song, this is fucking queer music. And this, I'm wearing fucking queer clothes. And this is fucking queer love.

I'm queer. You're queer. We're queer. And it's

The best. It's the fucking best.

He I'd quite like a kitchen island.

They But that's them. And we're. Oh, babe, we're so much –

He Better?

They You think so too?

He I'm going to bed

They *dances, and the music grows and grows into:*

A Day Before

They Uh oh

He Don't

They UH OH

He DON'T!

They Someone was druuuuuuuuunk

He Babe

They Someone was siiiiiiiiiiiiick

He On the floor

They On the throw

He Not from / the –

They // From the White Company. / Yeah, I know.

He // Nooooooooooooooooooooooooooo

No, no, no, no, no, no, no, no, no, / no, no, no, no, no, no, no

They // Don't worry it's fine I've –

He Yeah?

They Pink stuff. Fifty degrees.

He Fifty?!

They It's fine

He But what if it –

They It won't

He How do you–

They Last month I spilt nail varnish on it when you were working in / Oxford, and

He // Babe, nail varnish. What? / What? What the fu –

They // Because I sorted it and it was fine

Just like how I've sorted it today and it's going to be fine

He It is?

They Because I've sorted it

Because I'm amazing

He You are

They You were *wrecked*

He I still am

They Oh my drunkie boy

He I'm not a boy

They No?

He No

They Nooooooooo?

He Nooooooo, I'm a big sexy man

They A big sexy man, yeaaaaah

He Yeeeah, will you look after your big sexy man today, / pleeeeease?

They // Yessssssss, yes I can, and I will

He Oh babyyyyyyy, you're so good / to me

They // I know. I knoooooooooow. Do you want me to go get coffee?

Breakfast?

He No, no, no I want you to stay here with me

They Yeah?

He Look after / meeeee

They // Whiny man!

He I knooooow, so you can be *my* big sexy man today.

They Man?

He No, no, no, no, my boy. My big sexy boy. My sexy boy.

They Right

He Yeeeees, I need you to stay here. Pleeeeease

With me

They Okay. I will.

Two Months After

He We need to go and see my mum.

They Okay?

He And my stepdad.

They Right.

He Sorry, I'm, sorry, I know, I know but / we need to go, like –

They // Do you *need* me to come, could you go –

He My stepdad's in hospital.

They Oh my god.

Oh my god are you

Is he –

He I dunno, I just need to go and be, like, a good son, right now.

They What –

He And you need to go and be a good son-in-law, like right –

They Ah ah ah!

He Babe, now is not the time.

They Woaaaaaaahh –

He Babe, my mum is a mess.

They Okay, but you see what you –

He Mum's a mess, Kieran's in hospital and I think it's bad.

So can / we go?

They // Okay. Okay let's go.

* * * * *

He It just wasn't appropriate

They Appropriate? What the / fuck does that

He // He is in hospital!

They I know.

I was just telling him that I

How to –

He It wasn't about you though. Tonight. Was it?

Why could you not just deal with it, and then tell him, like, explain, next time we see him?

They Because I don't want to

To, to, to, to, *suit* certain

Like, I've had to all my life, other people's –

He So have I!

They It's different

He Is it?

They Yes. It is, because you look like how people want you to look.

He What?

They It doesn't matter. You don't understand.

He Then please try and explain to me what it is that I don't understand. Could you at least, please, just answer me that one simple fucking question, babe?

They You don't understand how much it hurts.

Because *everybody* gets it wrong. *All the time.*

Every Uber I get, 'Sir'. Every clothes shop is 'menswear'. Every announcement at the fucking theatre is 'ladies and gentlemen'.

So when I'm with you, and your, our

I at least expect to be able to –

He Okay, but how did you expect it would go? Arguing with him when he's lying in a fucking hospital gown? The man had a mini stroke, babe, what did you think was going to happen when you –

They I thought you would at least back me up.

And if you're not going to, then who is?

Exactly.

I have to do it myself.

He I can't get into this.

Not again, now.

They I don't enjoy it.

He What?

They Correcting.

Fighting. Every time.

Really I don't. Correcting your stepdad like I did tonight. Every time I have to do it, it's hell, actually.

All I can think about is what if . . . if they're going to laugh in my face? Tell me it's not real? Worse, punch me, beat me up. Actually, no laughing is probably worse. Because it's

Then it's like, they think all of this is not . . . like I've made it all up.

But I haven't. Do you think I have? Made this all up?

He Of course I don't think –

They Sometimes I'm not sure. Like tonight, when I wanted you to

He There's a time and a place, / babe and I . . .

They // But there's not, actually. For me there isn't, because this is who I am. It's not some *thing* that I'm just making up until the next trendy queer thing comes along. And if you truly understood that then I think you would have

Tonight.

It's who I am. Not what. Who.

And I *have* to be that person, even if it means I have to fight to be it,

I have to. And if you aren't going to help me fight then

He Then what?

Then what babe?

They I don't know.

He Fuck.

FUCK.

I wish you did babe. I really wish you did because a few years ago I fell in love with this man, who looked like you, sounded like you, even made all the same, silly, niche pop culture references as you.

And now that you know this, about

That you *are* changing

Do I have to pretend like he doesn't exist? Like he's dead?

Is he?

They I don't know

He FUCK. Why do you never

What if you never do?

They Well, I don't think I ever will if we keep / on like this

He // Keep on – what, are you saying we should just break up then?

Oh.

Oh.

Just like

Just, that's it?

And . . .

Just like that?

They 'And just like that, Big died'

He Oh *my* god

They Oh, god. I'm sorry, I'm trying to break the

He You're a fucking idiot!

They I know, I / know, I'm –

He // Fucking hell you just said that we're gonna break up and then you turn it into some stupid / fucking joke, I mean jesus.

They // I know, I'm sorry, I didn't mean to make it –

He I can't believe you're taking the piss when I

I really thought this was it. Forever.

They I thought so too. But maybe it never was. Maybe we were never going to –

He Really?

They I don't know.

He I wish you fucking did. That's what's made this all *so* hard, you know?

They So this is *my* fault?

He No, did I say that?

They Sort of, actually yes.

He Oh for fuck's

Even in our breakup you're pushing me, and being so

Fucking pedantic, / honest to fucking –

They // Pedantic? Wow, okay. Well I hope you'll be better off without me.

He Don't say that.

You know I don't think that. You know I can't bear the thought of

Of

I don't want you to

For this to be over.

They Okay.

He Okay?

They Yeah, okay. Well maybe then *you* can. Can

He Me?

They Well, yeah if you don't want this to end

He But you do? So why

They Yeah I don't think we should be

He So what are you saying?

They Well, I'm not the only person in this relationship. If you don't want to lose me, then why don't you fight for me?

He Are you serious?

They I just thought you would. It's a very you, very noble, romantic thing to do.

He What's the fucking point?

They Wow, okay so I'm / not *worth* fighting for? Wow, I –

He // I can't believe you're doing this!

They Well, I'm sad that this is ending too, and *yeah* I want to be fought for! / Why is that –

He // You're such a fucking drama / queen!

They // What the fuck? Gross. That's so fucking –

He I'm not fighting for you, because I think you're right.

You're right.

It kills me to say it, of course it fucking does, I adore you, but

You're right.

It's over.

And actually, yeah I think you're also right that it was probably always going to end. At some point. Maybe we were never

I dunno.

But it's over. Isn't it?

They Yeah. I think it is.

Yeah.

Twenty-Five Minutes Before

He Happy anniversary!

They Anni – what –

Babe! It's in like, a month?

He Ha, not this one!

They Oh.

Oh *right*. You naughty boy.

Oh my god. Is that –

It's a framed black and white picture of **They** *lying on a bed, naked, sleeping, semi wrapped in a bed sheet.*

Jesus, when did you? FUCK! YOU PERV!

He Surprise!

They Wow, I look fit.

He Right?

They I look like a Renaissance painting. But, like, a fit one.

I can't believe you never showed me this before!

He Well, look, I know you've been feeling like a bit, unconfident, unsexy and

Well, this is the person I remember sleeping with that very first night

I just want you to know how I saw you.

How I *still* see you. Every day.

The two of them kiss.

They I remember you called me beautiful a lot

He I still do, don't I?

They Sometimes

He Well, you are. Really fucking beautiful.

And I'm sorry if I don't say it often enough.

The two of them kiss again. It starts sort of sweet, but **They** *makes it a bit more wild and passionate.* **He** *breaks off and looks* **They** *directly in the eyes.*

Two Years After

They Oh shit

He Wow, yeah, god, hi

Jesus, it's been

They Yeah.

You look . . . . hot.

Sorry, I –

He No, don't be. I do? I – thanks. Thank you. Thanks.

Sorry, always awkward, / isn't it, when you . . .

They // No, *no,* it doesn't have to be . . .

Yeah. It is a bit. Isn't it?

He Yeah.

Sorry you, you look great too, you do

I'm just

You've been, I mean, you're in . . . a new

They Yeah

He How is he? Uhh, sorry, they?

They He.

He Right, he. How is – how is he?

They He's great.

He Is he better at it than I was?

They Mostly. But he makes mistakes too, sometimes.

He Oh, right.

I'm glad you're –

That's great.

They What about you?

He Just me.

They No, no, I saw on

You got / a

He // Oh, the dog, yeah.

A frenchie; such a cliche, I know but yeah. She's great.

She stinks but she's great.

They It's, honestly, it's really / nice to

He // Can I just say, something, please?

They Actually can I?

He Oh. Uhm.

Yeah? Sure. Go ahead.

They I think that maybe *I* expected *you* to

Too much, maybe. Too soon. And I do know that you tried. I really do know that. And I knew that then, I just was too caught up in

I'm sorry.

I know, now, that it's not all about . . . me.

He But the world is getting better at it, I think.

Do you think, that / the world is . . .

They // Yeah, oh yeah. I, yeah. I think it might be, yeah.

Ninety Seconds Before

The two of them are holding each other, post coital.

They What do you like about me?

He What?

They Like what do you *actually* like about me?

He I guess I've always admired how much you know yourself.

They Yeah?

He That first date, when we went to Five Guys and it was all a bit casual and cute, but even so do you remember what you did?

They Maybe?

He You *freaked* out because I paid for your meal. *Freaked* out.

They What?

He Yeah, you told me that you always *always* split the bill because you can't deal with upholding . . . I dunno, something about not being men and women

They Not wanting to uphold patriarchal practices, yeah

He Yeah. And I thought it was funny, how angry you got.

They Funny?

He Yeah but like, because it meant so much to you. It was cute. You know?

Over, what, a nine quid burger and fries? Like . . . the world was gonna end. It was, yeah, funny. Cute.

But mostly I thought . . . I remember thinking, wow, he knows who he is.

This is a boy who cares a lot about . . . *things.* Little things. But to him they're huge things. And I remember feeling that I was about to learn so much from you. And that made me . . . excited. And honestly babe, it still does.

Every. Single. Day.

They I have something I need to tell you.

End.

Methuen Drama Modern Plays

include

Bola Agbaje
Ayad Akhtar
Edward Albee
Jean Anouilh
John Arden
Peter Barnes
Clare Barron
Sebastian Barry
Alistair Beaton
Brendan Behan
Edward Bond
William Boyd
Bertolt Brecht
Howard Brenton
Amelia Bullmore
Anthony Burgess
Leo Butler
Jim Cartwright
Lolita Chakrabarti
Caryl Churchill
Lucinda Coxon
Tim Crouch
Shelagh Delaney
Ishy Din
Claire Dowie
David Edgar
David Eldridge
Dario Fo
Michael Frayn
John Godber
James Graham
David Greig
John Guare
Lauren Gunderson
Peter Handke
David Harrower
Jonathan Harvey
Robert Holman
David Ireland
Sarah Kane
Barrie Keeffe
Jasmine Lee-Jones
Anders Lustgarten
Duncan Macmillan
David Mamet
Patrick Marber
Martin McDonagh
Alistair McDowall
Arthur Miller
Tom Murphy
Phyllis Nagy
Anthony Neilson
Peter Nichols
Ben Okri
Joe Orton
Vinay Patel
Joe Penhall
Luigi Pirandello
Stephen Poliakoff
Lucy Prebble
Peter Quilter
Mark Ravenhill
Philip Ridley
Willy Russell
Sam Shepard
Martin Sherman
Chris Shinn
Jackie Sibblies Drury
Wole Soyinka
Simon Stephens
Kae Tempest
Laura Wade
Anne Washburn
Timberlake Wertenbaker
Roy Williams
Snoo Wilson
Theatre Workshop
Frances Ya-Chu Cowhig
Benjamin Zephaniah

Methuen Drama Contemporary Dramatists

include

John Arden (two volumes)
Arden & D'Arcy
Peter Barnes (three volumes)
Sebastian Barry
Mike Bartlett
Clare Barron
Brad Birch
Dermot Bolger
Edward Bond (ten volumes)
Howard Brenton (two volumes)
Leo Butler (two volumes)
Richard Cameron
Jim Cartwright
Caryl Churchill (two volumes)
Complicite
Sarah Daniels (two volumes)
Nick Darke
David Edgar (three volumes)
David Eldridge (two volumes)
Ben Elton
Per Olov Enquist
Dario Fo (two volumes)
Michael Frayn (four volumes)
John Godber (four volumes)
Paul Godfrey
James Graham (two volumes)
David Greig
John Guare
Lee Hall (two volumes)
Katori Hall
Peter Handke
Jonathan Harvey (two volumes)
Iain Heggie
Israel Horovitz
Declan Hughes
Terry Johnson (three volumes)
Sarah Kane
Barrie Keeffe
Bernard-Marie Koltès (two volumes)
Franz Xaver Kroetz
Kwame Kwei-Armah
David Lan
Bryony Lavery
Deborah Levy
Doug Lucie

Alistair MacDowall
Sabrina Mahfouz
David Mamet (six volumes)
Patrick Marber
Martin McDonagh
Duncan McLean
David Mercer (two volumes)
Anthony Minghella (two volumes)
Rory Mullarkey
Tom Murphy (six volumes)
Phyllis Nagy
Anthony Neilson (three volumes)
Peter Nichol (two volumes)
Philip Osment
Gary Owen
Louise Page
Stewart Parker (two volumes)
Joe Penhall (two volumes)
Stephen Poliakoff (three volumes)
David Rabe (two volumes)
Mark Ravenhill (three volumes)
Christina Reid
Philip Ridley (two volumes)
Willy Russell
Eric-Emmanuel Schmitt
Ntozake Shange
Sam Shepard (two volumes)
Martin Sherman (two volumes)
Christopher Shinn (two volumes)
Joshua Sobel
Wole Soyinka (two volumes)
Simon Stephens (five volumes)
Shelagh Stephenson
David Storey (three volumes)
C. P. Taylor
Sue Townsend
Judy Upton (two volumes)
Michel Vinaver (two volumes)
Arnold Wesker (two volumes)
Peter Whelan
Michael Wilcox
Roy Williams (four volumes)
David Williamson
Snoo Wilson (two volumes)
David Wood (two volumes)
Victoria Wood

Methuen Drama Student Editions

Alan Ayckbourn *Confusions* • **Mike Bartlett** *Earthquakes in London* • **Aphra Behn** *The Rover* • **Alice Birch** *Revolt. She Said. Revolt Again* • **Edward Bond** *Lear* • *Saved* • **Bertolt Brecht** *The Caucasian Chalk Circle* • *Fear and Misery in the Third Reich* • *The Good Person of Szechwan* • *Life of Galileo* • *Mother Courage and her Children* • *The Resistible Rise of Arturo Ui* • *The Threepenny Opera* • **Jon Brittain** *Rotterdam* • **Georg Büchner** *Woyzeck* • **Anton Chekhov** *The Cherry Orchard* • *The Seagull* • *Three Sisters* • *Uncle Vanya* • **Caryl Churchill** *Serious Money* • *Top Girls* • **Shelagh Delaney** *A Taste of Honey* • **Inua Ellams** *Barber Shop Chronicles* • **Euripides** *Elektra* • *Medea* • **Dario Fo** *Accidental Death of an Anarchist* • **Michael Frayn** *Copenhagen* • **John Galsworthy** *Strife* • **Nikolai Gogol** *The Government Inspector* • **Carlo Goldoni** *A Servant to Two Masters* • **James Graham** *This House* • **Tanika Gupta** *The Empress* • **Katori Hall** *The Mountaintop* • **Lorraine Hansberry** *A Raisin in the Sun* • **Robert Holman** *Across Oka* • **Henrik Ibsen** *A Doll's House* • *Ghosts* • *Hedda Gabler* • **Sarah Kane** *4.48 Psychosis* • *Blasted* • **Charlotte Keatley** *My Mother Said I Never Should* • **Dennis Kelly** *DNA* • **Bernard Kops** *Dreams of Anne Frank* • **Federico García Lorca** *Blood Wedding* • *Doña Rosita the Spinster* (bilingual edition) • *The House of Bernarda Alba* (bilingual edition) • *Yerma* (bilingual edition) • **David Mamet** *Glengarry Glen Ross* • *Oleanna* • **Patrick Marber** *Closer* • **John Marston** *The Malcontent* • **Martin McDonagh** *The Lieutenant of Inishmore* • *The Lonesome West* • *The Beauty Queen of Leenane* • *The Cripple of Inishmaan* • **Alistair McDowall** *Pomona* • **John McGrath** *The Cheviot, the Stag and the Black, Black Oil* • **Arthur Miller** *All My Sons* • *The Crucible* • *A View from the Bridge* • *Death of a Salesman* • *The Price* • *After the Fall* • *The Last Yankee* • *A Memory of Two Mondays* • *Broken Glass* • *Incident at Vichy* • *The American Clock* • *The Ride Down Mt. Morgan* • **Joe Orton** *Loot* • **Joe Penhall** *Blue/Orange* • **Luigi Pirandello** *Six Characters in Search of an Author* • **Lucy Prebble** *Enron* • **Mark Ravenhill** *Shopping and F***ing* • **Reginald Rose** *Twelve Angry Men* • **Willy Russell** *Blood Brothers* • *Educating Rita* • **Lemn Sissay** Benjamin Zephaniah's *Refugee Boy* • **Sophocles** *Antigone* • *Oedipus the King* • **Wole Soyinka** *Death and the King's Horseman* • **Simon Stephens** *Punk Rock* • *Pornography* • **Shelagh Stephenson** *The Memory of Water* • **August Strindberg** *Miss Julie* • **J. M. Synge** *The Playboy of the Western World* • **Kae Tempest** *Wasted* • **Theatre Workshop** *Oh What a Lovely War* • **Laura Wade** *Posh* • **Frank Wedekind** *Spring Awakening* • **Timberlake Wertenbaker** *Our Country's Good* • **Arnold Wesker** *The Merchant* • **Peter Whelan** *The Accrington Pals* • **Oscar Wilde** *The Importance of Being Earnest* • **Roy Williams** *Sing Yer Heart Out for the Lads* • **Tennessee Williams** *A Streetcar Named Desire* • *The Glass Menagerie* • *Cat on a Hot Tin Roof* • *Sweet Bird of Youth*

www.ingramcontent.com/pod-product-compliance
Lightning Source LLC
LaVergne TN
LVHW010938110826
845149LV00013B/2665

* 9 7 8 1 3 5 0 6 3 3 7 4 2 *